Dad,

Hope this book brings back happy memories of Ireland. I enjoyed looking through it - realizing and appreciating the wild beauty of my heritage.

My Love to You.

Shannon Ann

THE COTTAGES & CASTLES OF IRELAND

THE COTTAGES & CASTLES OF IRELAND

Commentary
SANDY LESBERG

PEEBLES PRESS
New York   London

FIRST PUBLISHED 1976 BY
PEEBLES PRESS INTERNATIONAL
12 Thayer St., London W1M 5LD
10 Columbus Circle, New York, N.Y. 10019

Designed by Nicolai Canetti

© Peebles Press International (Europe) Ltd
ISBN 0–672–52221–7
Library of Congress Catalog No. 75–36327

The publishers wish to acknowledge with great gratitude the splendid assistance
and co-operation they have received in the preparation of this book
from the Irish Tourist Board.

Distributed by
The Bobbs-Merrill Co. Inc.
4300 West 62nd St., Indianapolis, Indiana 46268, U.S.A
in the United States and Canada

WHS Distributors
Euston St., Freemen's Common, Leicester, England
in the U.K., Ireland, Australia, New Zealand and South Africa

Meulenhoff-Bruna B.V.
Beulingstraat 2, Amsterdam, Netherlands
in the Netherlands

Printed and bound in the U.K. by
Redwood Burn Limited, Trowbridge and Esher

The thing to remember about Ireland is that you must not jumble up the fantasies with the realities. Here is the one place on earth where the shadows can sometimes be as strong as the substance which might well be hazy and blurred and not quite well defined, and where you don't have to be exactly certain that what you've just seen or heard is really today's hard fact or merely a snippet of yesterday's echo.

Ireland is where simplicity and grandeur are all mixed up in a wondrous, singular coming together that defies definition and is more felt than observed. It's there in the land, and in the people, and flows with gentle force everywhere you travel, making you feel that everyone you meet could well be at least an ancient Irish nobleman if not a simple wandering minstrel. It's a unique feeling, all over Ireland.

Here on the western fringe of Europe, on this land surrounded by sea and played the fool by the winds, for 8,000 years men from all over the globe have wandered and rooted and spawned bits and pieces of their culture that have evolved into today's free Republic. Surely now it has its own face, its own sound, its own people – but there are somehow always the rumblings in the background of the Celts (taller than Roman spears), the Danes, the Normans (who became more Irish than the Irish themselves), the British and even the French.

The Normans were the first castle builders, back in the early 13th century. They founded many monasteries to protect themselves against the devil and then with medieval pragmatism erected equally as many fortified edifices to protect themselves against their more worldly foes. Very few of these early castles survive but some have been incorporated into later buildings. Many remain, however, from the 15th and 16th centuries and can still be seen in one state or another. But never mind their physical condition. If you keen your eyes and *see* them, rather than just look at them, you will observe the lord of the manor being served his mead and mutton at the long, wooden banquet table while dancers and lyre players amuse him and themselves in the background. A brace of wolf hounds lie at his feet, snapping at what he deigns to toss them, while his lady sits by his side. The great, high stone walls are warmed by the flame flickering in the enormous fireplace that occupies half the north wall. He is content at his evening meal. He knows his armour has been shined and is even now hanging in his sleeping room a mere few stone steps up from where he dines. Thus it was in the year 1250, or perhaps it is even now. It all depends on whether you are prepared to deal with the shadows.

Modern Ireland is dotted with many recently constructed and much more modest homesteads – the thatched, white cottages that are no less the province of a contemporary lord of the manor, admittedly less endowed with worldly goods and I suspect quite a bit less embattled than his forebears. But even though the thatched cottage could well fit physically into the great dining hall of many a castle, the central focal point of both is the same – the massive fireplace. Many of the cottages have such wide fireplaces that the entire family can and often does sit in under the chimney around the turf fire.

They each contribute to the fabric of Ireland, these cottages and castles, and in no sense can one be judged more vital nor more contemporary than the other. The castles are for dreaming and the cottages are for living, but some say that the dreams of yesterday contribute mightily to the living of today. Being Ireland, it's sometimes hard to separate the dreams from the reality of living.

This cottage has its roof thatching pegged-down to resist the storms which blow in from the Atlantic in the winter.

Cottage at Annestown near Tramore, County Waterford.

Curracloe, County Wexford. Two boys leaving for a walk with their dogs.

Renvyle, Connemara, County Galway.

Couminole, Dingle Penninsula, County Kerry. A summer view of the cottage shown on page 6.

A Donegal cottage.

A Connemara cottage.

Dunmore East, County Waterford.

Glencar, County Kerry.

Adare, County Limerick.

The ancient art of roof thatching in County Clare.

Ballaghkeen in County Wexford. Population 130,
some of whom utilize an ancient and honorable form of transport.

OVERLEAF   Lough Corrib, Doon, near Oughterard, Connemara, County Galway.

County Donegal.

Curracloe, County Wexford. Two boys returning from a walk with their dogs.

County Cavan.

A Donegal cottage.

Mannin and the Twelve Bens,
Ballyconneely, Connemara, County Galway.

Two Donegal cottages.

Near Kenmare, County Kerry.

County Galway.

County Longford.

County Galway.

Connemara, County Galway.

Bunratty Folk Park, County Clare.

Near Listowel, County Kerry.

Dunguaire Castle, County Galway.

Lackeen Castle, Abbeville, County Tipperary.

Burncourt, County Tipperary.

Coolehull, County Wexford.

Classiebawn, County Sligo.

Dromoland Castle, Newmarket-on-Fergus, County Clare.

Part of the lobby of Dromoland Castle, which has been recently converted into an extremely comfortable country hotel.

Classiebawn Castle, County Sligo.

Carrick-on-Suir Castle, County Tipperary.

Craggannowen Castle, County Clare.

Lismore Castle, County Waterford.

Knapague Castle, County Clare.

Nemagh Castle, Nemagh, County Tipperary.

Two views of Trim Castle, Manorland, County Meath.

Ballintober, County Roscommon.

Aughnanure, County Galway.

Dunsany, County Meath.

Castlecooke, County Cork.

Shanbally, County Tipperary.

Donegal.

Lohort, County Cork.

Greencastle, County Donegal.

Dunsany, County Meath.

Some ancient bas reliefs found in Ballynacarriga Castle, County Cork.

Medieval Banquets are held in several restored castles.

Annaghdown, County Galway.

Conna, County Cork.

Carrigafoyle, County Kerry.

RIGHT   Roscrea, County Tipperary.

OVERLEAF   Johnstown Castle, County Wexford.

Round Castle, Parkavonear, County Kerry.

Ormonde Castle, Kilkenny City, County Kilkenny.

90

Doe Castle, Castledoe, County Donegal.

Medieval music, pageantry and feasting
in a reconstructed castle.

Mediaeval heads at Bargy, County Wexford.

Lohort, County Cork.

Barleycove.

Clogherhead, County Louth.

Killiney, County Dublin.

Doe Castle, Castledoe, County Donegal.

A County Cork castle dating back to about 1600.

Liscarroll, County Cork.

Dromoland Castle at night.

Carlow Castle, from the 13th century. The other half was blown up in the
early 19th century, to make way for an institution.

Blackrock Castle, County Cork.

Burnchurch Tower, County Kilkenny.

The rock of Cashel.

Lohort Castle, County Cork.

Johnstown Castle, County Wexford.

Tower of Castle, Leighlinbridge, County Carlow.

Dromoland Castle, from the air.

Trim Castle, County Meath.

Putley Hall, Castletownbeere, County Cork.

OVERLEAF   Dromoland Castle.